Dreaming at the Wheel

dreaming
at
the wheel

by

Charles Behlen

1988

Library of Congress Catalog No. 88-70159
ISBN 0-931722-49-7

Cover illustration adapted from "American Temple No. 1"
by Jim Stoker. Cover design by Brian Schill.

Printed and bound in the United States of America

Many of these poems first appeared, often in slightly different versions, in the following periodicals, anthologies, chapbooks and pamphlet, for which grateful acknowledgment is given:

Aileron, The Bloomsbury Review, Cedar Rock, Crawlspace, The New Mexico Humanities Review, The Pawn Review, Pax, Poetry Motel, Poetry Now, Puerto del Sol, The Greater Llano Estacado Southwest Heritage, Stone Drum, University of Houston Voice

Anthology of Magazine Verse and Yearbook of American Poetry / 1985 edition (Alan Pater, editor and publisher; Monitor Book Co., 1985) "The Voices"

Anthology of Magazine Verse and Yearbook of American Poetry / 1986-87 edition (Alan Pater, editor and publisher; Monitor Book Co., 1987) "The Drunk's Widow"

Christmas in Texas (Helen Williams and V.T. Abercrombie, editors; Brown Rabbit Press, 1979) "Christmas Eve / Lubbock, Texas"

Crossing the River (Ray Gonzalez, editor; The Permanent Press, 1987) "On the Plains, in West Texas—"

Flights South (Charles Behlen, editor; Cultural Council of Victoria, 1987) "He was Dead—"

From Hide and Horn (Peggy Zuleika Lynch and Edmund Lynch, editors; Eakin Press, 1985) "Two Ice Storms"

Images from the High Plains (Gerald Craven, editor; Staked Plains Press, 1979) "Grandfather Encountered in Elmwood Cemetery" and "Widow Zebach"

Three Texas Poets (Dave Oliphant, editor and publisher; Prickly Pear Press, 1986) "Uirsche Contemplates Eternity and the Productions of Time," "The Last Address of My Maternal Grandfather," and "Tornado"

Washing the Cow's Skull / Lavando la Calavera de Vaca (Dave Oliphant and Luis Ramos-Garcia, editors and publishers; Prickly Pear Press / Studia Hispanica Editors, 1981) "The Death of Whitman"

"My Grandfather's Hammer," "Elegy for Paula" and "Dreaming Back to the Barrio / 1954" first appeared in *My Grandfather's Hammer* (Ray Gonzalez, editor and publisher; Mesilla Press Pamphlet Series #11, 1985)

Thirteen of these poems appeared in *I Am Part Of All That I Have Met* (Chawed Rawzin Chapbook Series #5, 1984)

All of the Uirsche Poems in the present volume appeared in *Uirsche's First Three Decades* (Del Marie Rogers, editor and publisher; Firewheel Press, 1987)

CONTENTS

ONE

Two Ice Storms 8
Uirsche Contemplates Eternity and the Productions of Time 10
Rex 11
Father Encountered Drunk Under a Bridge 13
Uirsche Evokes His Dead Father—— 14
On the Plains, in West Texas—— 15
Dogs 16
Uirsche's Adolescence 18
Martha Brunner 19
My Grandfather's Hammer 21
The Last Address of My Maternal Grandfather 22
The Voices 24
Grandfather Encountered in Elmwood Cemetery 26

TWO

Given Ground 28
He was Dead—— 29
Farm Auction Near Tatum, New Mexico / 1968 30
Widow Zebach 31
Zella Matney Talking at the Family Reunion 32
The Drunk's Widow 36
Dreaming at the Wheel 38

THREE

The Death of Whitman 40
A Shark in a Cadillac 41
Tornado 42
Christmas Eve / Lubbock, Texas 44
At Crosbie's / Acuña 45
Men Waking 47

FOUR

When You Took Your Luggage——	50
Older	50
Elegy for Paula	51
Calming My Daughter	52
Night-watching with My Daughter	53
Uirsche Endures a Weariness that Passes All Understanding	54

FIVE

Uirsche on Circling	56
Dreaming Back to the Barrio / 1954	58

for Laura

ONE

Two Ice Storms

Between contractions,
my mother dreamed
of black water,
a lake by a road
I fell in and fell in.
She'd reach shoulder-deep,
feel my small hand slipping
down and away, and
startle awake to the
hospital radiator
crackling its spine,
the crazed wind
glazing everything.

So I was born wet and cold,
my cradle tipped
by an iced howl
I never forgot.

On the edge of the Caprock,
where the prairie drops
its glacial face to a
warm, rolling south,
I wrapped frozen pipes
while a deer carcass creaked
from the wellhouse rafter,
creaked and swung its
bloodied shoulders
against my breath.
The sights of my 12-gauge
held miles of prairie;
held the alert, empty
eye-thoughts of rabbits;

held the buried light
of Cherokee flint;
held the fast hearts
of wintered sparrows.
And the sky's mouth
held my life,
thawless and grinding
an edge of the Caprock.

When the Great Storm of '62
closed the school early,
I tramped the miles home
through ice-stubbled acreage
and cut ice from the
door with a hoe.

Inside, the rooms
were chilled brittle,
waiting.

I huddled with a pot
of bitter coffee,
braced, pushed, and
dropped out of childhood.

Uirsche Contemplates Eternity and the Productions of Time

Let's say your father abandons your mother
for the far towns, their money and women,
and she spends the next thirty-five years
in a school cafeteria in Brinks County, Texas.

And let's say, as she spoons mashed potatoes
onto heavy, white plates and hands them down,
she pictures herself in a tight, blue dress,
in a furnished room with starched, clean sheets.

The man who is paying is fresh and kind.
As he moves to embrace her he sees her eyes
and the goodness there stops and shames him.
He remembers when he was ten years old

and watched the stars pale in the morning.
He falls to his knees, begs marriage, forgiveness,
and the sun lifts out of the brand-new land
of their happy future. Let's say

in the clash and steam of metal trays
your mother dreamed this. She kept this story
for the hours when she needed it most
and awoke one morning in her old age
to the last heavy, white plate of her life.

Rex

Old dog dead for
twenty-five years,
you're back again and
drag your hindlegs
through my dreams.

Last night, summer
swarmed again on the
hot backporch where,
passive and patient,
you stood while the tweezers
danced in the aperture
in your back leg,
danced while the screw worms
tunneled past,
a rapid transit
wrecking muscle, nerve.
Caught, each worm was
dropped in a jar
of gasoline,
flexed twice and settled
to the bottom.

We worked until the
summer night went
deaf in our ears,
but, by morning,
the legs were sticks
you dragged to your bowl.

When the policeman
whistled you
into his backseat,
ashamed, obedient,
and afraid, you
steadied your forelegs,
did what you could.

Father Encountered Drunk Under a Bridge

When you took a piss
in Horse Shoe Creek
and ambled downstream
to wash your face
we both had to laugh.
Years lost between us,
you cocked your head
to my voice,
announced it
"Californian."
We giggled at
the dirty words
on the underbelly
of the bridge,
took turns on your crazy
German accordion.
That scared the swallows
(or whatever was nesting
in those mud tenements);
they shot out screaming,
spilled the beer.

Yes, that was once.
We liked each other.

Uirsche Evokes His Dead Father—

and the ghost swoons up through him like nausea.
He props the old man in the family car,
jams a two-by-four between gas pedal and seat,
smiles and waves as the car works off
to the canyon of Hoped-for Amnesia.
But the car doubles back into Uirsche's life.
He catches the stench of his father's breath,
sees spit in his mouth gleam in the dashlights
as the father hollers his Old Testament God
from a Bible skewered on the steering-column.
Uirsche leaps for the keys, tumbles to the backseat
as the car plows down Mom and the kids
where they stand, mired to their waists in the marriage.
The car stops for a blonde, stops for a brunette.
Their mascaraed eyes drool like wounds.
Their lipsticked mouths mime their crazed lives.
Lice in their clothes tick like watches;
tick faster, faster to the whirr of the motor
as the car circles back to the edge.
Uirsche weeps, flashes cards he has crayoned with
snow on roses in the diningroom window;
the baths in his father's dark, big hands;
accordions swaying on backyard porches.
But they melt into Rorschachs.
Blitzed by years of pills and wine,
the brains behind his father's eyes
stare back for his death.
Uirsche sees the mouth pull open,
sees beetles roving under the eyelids,
reaches for the door,
whispers "goodbye."

On the Plains, in West Texas—

the deer hung from the wellhouse rafter
where it twisted, frozen and alone
through the push of wind,
the prairie winter.

When the white geese threaded out of the south;
when the chain on the flagless schoolhouse pole
broke free and whipped the cool air warmer;
when the ugly elms rashed mint green
and the March gusts burned the dust to the air,

I was given this:

to pry the wellhouse open with a hoe.
If the carcass was cold there was meat for three weeks.
If the neck-stump dripped maggots on the floor
I cut the deer loose, dragged it to the field
and doused it with gas.

While the body burned open
I stood among the broken-necked stalks,
felt the sky change course as the
geese trawled softly for a darker home.

Dogs

There was a small one
that coughed froth
and two big ones
(a brother and sister),
their piss-yellow hair
matted by days of
sleepy indigence.
They lived that way,
napping under my
grandmother's house,
panhandling for scraps,
milling the porch.

When he came to kill them,
my uncle laid
the 12-gauge
across his wide lap
and finished a beer.
My grandmother waited
under the wall phone,
fingers in ears,
eyes shut tight
and shouted
SIT DOWN AND BE QUIET
as I jumped from
window to window
and the soft pops
jostled the china.

A big yellow one
lay on the road.
Its tail still wagged,
thrashed the gravel.
The others soaked
two gunnysacks in the
back of the pickup.

While my grandmother
patted sweat
from the sixpack,
my uncle let me
shovel sand on the
moons of blood.

There was a buckshot wound
in the side of the wellhouse.
I fingered it, dreamed
of earning my keep.

Uirsche's Adolescence

While the wind stitched and cried against a house trailer
        in West Texas cotton;
while dust smothered the centerfolds snarled in
        railroad weeds;
while shotguns bucked across prairie snow;
while his mother sweated in dime store aisles for $50 a week;
while his grandmother read his teenage wastage on the pillows
        and sheets
and wept from a black, thick book called *Christian Health*,
and the fields tilted into 1960,
and the wind howled out its homesickness for the '30s,
this boy Uirsche
drank Coke from a Jim Beam fifth,
clung to the deer carcass hanging in the wellhouse,
and swaggered forth like his father.

Martha Brunner

Small, bespectacled bird,
at eighty-six you
lost for good the
uncomfortable English,
dreamed outloud in
childhood German.
When you didn't stop,
we pushed your chair
to the nursing home.
Now, the disinfectant
deep in your lungs,
you sing in sleep "The
Hamburg Departure;"
the sky on the sea,
its promise: America;
the customs inspector
on Ellis Island
who shouted dog noises
and fumbled a breast
along with your bundles.

You play-act in sleep.
Your hands go out to the
crumbling walls of the
root cellar where an
Illinois farmer
stored you at night
along with the onions.
Then you weep and smile
for the old Czech couple

who pulled you from the dark,
who brought you up
to Shiner, Texas.

You dream awake, ever
since your sleep deepened,
of the Dust Bowl '30s
when you shoveled sand
from your barren kitchen.
You weep for the child
the newspaper said
was caught and killed
by the first big blow
in Hays County, Kansas;
you weep for the rabbits,
the small birds smothered
by the dark air.

Frau Martha, when your
hands X your breasts
it will be for the years
of your husband's silence
when you joined the church.
When your hands X your lap
it will be for the years
of your husband's silence
when you bore the third child.

Frau Martha, when those
hands fall silent
it will be for the sons
who shot the buds
from your rosebush;
it will be for the sons

who wiped their boots
on the shirts you scrubbed
and ironed for hours.

Frau Martha, the sons
who left you and the plains
began with you there.
Give us the ending
of your story.
It is our
beginning.

My Grandfather's Hammer

A hard head.
A straight back.
When I tossed it down
it kicked the dirt
curtly,
slept at attention
like a Prussian.
Its voice was the
cry of a nail
clawed from a plank,
the gripe of a coin
pried from an acre
of Texas cotton
from 1918
to 1957.

The Last Address of My Maternal Grandfather

Like a loaf of resurrected sidewalk
the wet cement shone in the daylight as
I wobbled up on my year-old legs and
stared as my father spelled with his hands
your name and year in dime store tin.

And there it stood: a homemade headstone.
A proper monument to a man who
left his kin one Czech cowbell,
one copper ashtray shaped like a Stetson
and one wrecked novel called *Saint Elmo*.

Like a loaf of bread on a summer lawn,
an old head napping at a church picnic, it was
lifted to the trunk of my father's DeSoto,
spirited off to the little streets
of Elmwood Memorial.

Throughout my childhood the
bright tin glinted your name and year
at the passing weather.
On summer visits your mound felt hot.
I would touch the bare ground and
think of you simmering through
airconditionless eternities.
When the tail of a snake flicked down a hole
I cringed for you.

As the grownups circled your stone
I squinted and saw you grinning home,
your thin arms brimming with trinkets
from the South Plains Fair
while the sky darkened with the Depression.
While your kin hacked at their acre of corn,
I saw you on the porch of a shack
wheezing out the "Blue Skirt Waltz"
on a patched and winded concertina.

Keen Vincent Brake, death to a child is a
lonely place where they won't let you play.
I squinted again and saw you
kept after class in the long school of years.

Time has pried the dime store tin
from the face of your stone,
but the imprints whisper in their shadows:
"Stay with this foolish child a while longer.
The waves of dust roll us under, over."

The Voices

As each stroke fell through your brain
you gripped your son's hands—
clinched and worked.
You seemed to be dreaming of the
cows you milked for forty-five years.

Miles away, I walked your farm,
watched a patch of snow in
a dead snarl of weeds
wither to air.
I thought of the stillborn,
flecks too pure to
stand the daylight.

Seventy years of wind and sun
had blackened the workshed,
blackened it like the soil where
generations of barnyard dung
stung the earth so rich
it burned the young corn,
curled the Swiss chard.

In the attic I found a box of books
from my father's childhood—
their bright covers open,
innocent as a nursery.
But the bindings were mauled,
bruised black and green
by a swarm of termites.

                                Sickened,
I fell back on my heels and
sprayed the pages with disinfectant.
The house stank for days
with a heavy sweetness.

Grandfather, your hands
have worked past my eyes
to a spectrum of light
I cannot yet follow.
I talk to your big-faced radio,
fidget with the dials,
curse and listen.
It arches before me
like a tombstone.
It crackles. The voices
seem to be burning.
The signal smolders
to a patient silence
that will last forever.

Grandfather Encountered in Elmwood Cemetery

The wind points the grass another way
where I find you hiding under a stone
that is knee-high, like the kitchen chairs
you edged around when I played "hide-and-seek."
You never found me, you never looked.
You stared out to your fields for rain.
Now I stand overhead and search for my car.
Our eyes cannot meet and we have no words
where the grass, your grass, points another way.

TWO

Given Ground

1 (How to tell when you are in West Texas)

Look up.
That's the sky.
Look down.
That's the ground.
Now look straight ahead.
See how the two just stare at each other?
They've been married forever.
They hate it.
They are too old to divorce.
They take it out on the children.

2 (How to make a West Texan)

Cross an Eskimo
with a Hawaiian.
The offspring will look
like Apaches,
hack igloos out of
the flat, hard earth.
Their hula will gesture
twenty words for wind,
twenty words for dust,
forty words for chafe,
end with double negatives.

He was Dead—

in the eyes, I mean.
His overalls flapped
like a gray flag
as he strode in my store
and threw on his back
a ten pound sack
of Goldmedal flour.
When he turned for the door
I yelled THAT FLOUR
COSTS FIFTY-FIVE CENTS.
That's when I saw
he was dead in the eyes:
his stare pushed me back
and I bumped a display
of Farm/Sport Socks.
Yes, I called the law.
It's been forty-odd years
but, you know, some nights
I still wake up sorry.
But the sheriff just parked
up the road, propped
his ass on the hood and
held onto his Stetson.
We watched his wife and kids
drive their arms deep
into the ripped sack
and slap the dry handfuls
into their mouths.
Then we watched the old guy
crank his truck,
his Texas plates
disappear in the dust
and the white sack tumble
out to the fields—
and got back to work.

Farm Auction Near Tatum, New Mexico / 1968

It has taken my eyes years to see
how I leaned against your rusting tractor,
snapped gum beneath my John Deere feedcap.
It has taken my eyes years to learn
how the rifle waited on the pickup window;
how the heft of its company
on the lonely walks through the windbreaks of trees
was a final friendship; how, set adrift,
you gripped this oar while
fathoms of debt heaved beneath you and,
when you looked to it for an answer,
how it stared back, alert with exact usage.

While the auctioneer throttled what remained of your life
        in the fists of his voice,
I could have thumped my gum on the kitchen window,
charged admission where the acids in your blood
dulled the linoleum.
                                I could have barked
LADIES AND GENTLEMEN, SEE HOW A MAN POURS
ALL HE IS INTO ALL HE OWNS AND LOSES BOTH.
        But I was twenty—
empty of loss as the shadows of clouds
that claimed and lost the acres of maize.

It has taken years and the loss of
children, teeth, house keys and hair
to drive me back to your scarred wristwatch,
the broken work boots leaning in the hall,
the cold stacks of *Field and Stream* in the
        stilled, airless bedroom.
It has taken years to tell you: Alvin Caldwell,
the grains of dust that grit my eyes are
        seeds of remembrance.
You have repossessed what possessed you.

Widow Zebach

Off Interstate 20
she whirls her hoe
the acreage now
a bedroom wall
a six foot
stand of weeds
Husband dead
(a farming mishap)
both sons dead
("Nam" Korea)
the house lost to
a lightning fire in
'68 and she
whirls her hoe
It lifts and
disappears
lifts
disappears
in the sun
in the moon
The relatives pass
at 70 yelling
GIVE IT UP BEATRICE
The weeds keep working
at that one
charred wall
remaining

Zella Matney Talking at the Family Reunion

How we held each other
those last howling nights
in Brinks County, Texas.
The dust seeped through
the bedroom windows,
terraced the sheets,
cut our shins.
Boy, let me tell you,
that lullaby rocked me
right out of the cradle.
I found myself lashed
to a flat-bed truck,
growing up by the mile
through Dalhart, Wink,
through Sweetwater, Texas.
First day out
the dust in my eyes
turned to mud and the
mud turned to stones that
the wind slapped away
and tossed to the fields.
As the truck bucked off
I stared back to the place
where the dust and road
got lost in the dark
and shivered in my
thin print dress at
a roar I took for
the voice of the Lord

telling us Matneys
to get the hell out.

Then those boiling summers
near Leonard, Texas.
From the hot, still shade
of Keen's front porch
we watched the scud clouds
sharpen to twisters
while Pearl just sat,
big arms folded,
gray hair down
across her scowl and
said we "was actin'
scared over nuthin'."
So thin from bouts of
tuberculosis they
nick-named me "Skeeter,"
I'd help haul Pearlie
to the cellar where
we'd hunker in the stink
of onions and dirt,
cock our heads for the
high-pitched whistle
of passing cyclones.
Night after night
in the cramped, stale dark,
my mind far away on
Frank charging sandhills
on Okinawa,
I sat staring up
as the cross-tie beams

kept the world off our heads.
We sang "Rock of Ages,"
sang "Love Lifted Me,"
while the young ones cried
and Keen cussed a streak
as he held the door shut
with a knotted rope.
Then one morning we
crawled up to the sun.
The first thing I saw
was the sky through Jesse's
bedroom window, then
the milk cow lying
out in the field with
a board through her side.
The chintz curtains thrashed
from the busted windows,
brushed the hoe handles
leaning on the porch.
Keen's Ford pickup,
the house, you-name-it,
all plastered with a
stucco of mud from
a rain lake over
in Hockley County,
and Pearl just stands,
arms folded, and says
"Now *that's* how I like it
when I've slept in a cellar."
Boy, let me tell you,
you should've known her.

It's been forty-odd years
but I keep an ear tuned

to the wind while I sleep.
And if my dreams catch
a certain pitch in the wind
my knees roam the sheets
for the remembered grit.
Now keep this to yourself:
with the first spring storm,
the first fall duster,
I sleepwalk the house
and raise all the windows.
When Frank was alive
he'd hear me bang
into a wall and
he'd say "Zella,
I wish you'd stop that,"
and I'd wake up and say
"Frank, so do I."
Now all it takes is
the night roar of
a Santa Fe freight
and I'm up sleepwalking,
raising windows.
I wake up and wait
for Frank's "I wish . . ."
then I wake up some more
and remember he's gone.
I stand in the dark,
smile out to the dark.
I know that's where I'm going.

The Drunk's Widow

My cats must think the
housepainter's Landis;
they scatter when he
drags up his ladder.
Today, I'll rummage
in the cellar.
Can't stand this house
when the painter hammers
back the nails that
Landis beat loose
for thirty-five years.
Thirty-five years of
ten-penny nails
torture each other
in a dozen Mason
jars down there and
a jumbled marriage of
saws and drills lies
rusting in Jim Beam
crates down there.
I've got to forget, as
I dream through his rooms,
how the three Sunday suits
hang empty of him as
they did in his life;
how the dumb boots, split
by his thick ankles,
lean in the hallway.
I'll give them to the painter
if he washes this
whiskey-yellowed house
back to white.

When I pulled in the drive
after morning Mass
the June sun burned on
the front of my house
and I felt cleansed.
Once Landis and me
were a secret kept
bright behind doors.
Then the howling whiskey-
fits of his rage made
us everyone's talk.
I like this white.
When it flares through me
my husband's ribs lock
cleanly with mine in
the good and secret
dark again.

Dreaming at the Wheel

A cowboy in
a '65 Olds
dives off a cliff
into Buffalo Canyon.
Months later, kids
out camping with the folks,
play Buck Rogers in
the gnarled, burnt metal,
grip the controls
and rollercoaster
down time warps to
a dozen black holes.
Sucked pure of light, they
play dead and run back
to hotdogs and Mom.
At night the wrecked car
orbits their sleep
like a black sun and,
beneath their heads,
earth wheels them along
on the ride of their lives.
They jerk half awake,
lunge for the controls
and hurtle down.

THREE

The Death of Whitman

When your face went easy
into all that white
on the hottest, stillest
day in Camden, the
great, shining arms of
the engine yard anvilled
your departure.
When I think of the iron,
the sweating still
of '92,
I remember the brakeman
I saw as a boy:
naked to the waist,
he walked off a boxcar
doing 30, just
stepped down
with easy strides and
ambled to the switch.

A Shark in a Cadillac—

was picking his teeth with
a mint-tipped toothpick.
"Listen," he said,
I sell skin diving gear for
a firm out of Houston.
I'm 24, 6 foot 2,
and in another 5 years
I'll pull 50 grand as
district manager for
the Gulf Coast region."

This shark had a 40 buck
"swept back" haircut.
It waved like black seaweed,
waved like he was driving
fast under water.

His day-old beard was
a thousand black points.
Each point was a kill in
the skin diving business
across the jaw of Texas.

When he dropped me out
he snapped the toothpick,
flipped it at me and said
"When I get into town
I'm going to shower, shave,
and cruise a few bars
for a piece of butt."

Then he shifted into drive,
filled the dark miles ahead
with the hood of his car.

TORNADO

The radio yells
TORNADO ON GROUND
AT EAST 19TH—
then statics out.
A desk clerk at
the Muremba Motel,
I grip the formica
as Al, the fat,
bald manager
runs in and shouts
we should take cover
under the stairs.
But the switchboard
has warned me:
Al wears pantyhose,
likes to be whipped,
so I lash myself
to the Coke machine
with the telephone cord
and shout above
the flapping roof:
AN HONEST PRODUCT,
AN HONEST DEATH.
Al shrieks and dives
for the men's room.
The panelling buckles,
the switchboard writhes
like a Medusa.
Then I see it,
I see it, through
the MasterCharge stickers
on the plateglass window:

God's hooked phallus
bull-tongue plowing
up East 19th,
churning up trees
with Monte Carlos,
typhooning Clap Park's
Maxine Lake and
slinging debris on
the brand-new dorms
of Texas Tech.
Then everything blows
like a dropped chandelier.
The air jet-engines
out the window.
The Coke machine dances me
through the lightning.
I hear Al scream,
a condom machine
ricochet off tile.
Torn from the floor,
the office twists upward
through the funneled distance
and I read Al's thighs
in the dark, moving sky:

Sheer Miss
Size Medium-Large
Mocha Brown

christmas eve / lubbock texas

silent night
silent night
our children leave
their dead asleep

they leap the lawns
drunkenly decked
with discount christs

and dodge the boas
of tinsel flapping
from the streetlamps

their voices pinging
on the hot dusty wind
the lids of our beds
sliding shut

At Crosbie's / Acuña

Beyond the frosted glass,
the rich finishes
of Crosbie's Restaurant,
thin kids hound touristas
with garlic ropes,
flags of lace,
and a shawled woman
sways through traffic,
one palm up while the
other pats a nursing child.

At Crosbie's the Tecate
and Pollo Portugesa
take quite a while.
Standing,
I drift along walls
decked with photos
of the Revolution:
grainy, ancient instants
of Pancho, Emillo
lounging on the grass
like overfed uncles;
of General Huerta,
stiff and old behind
his funny sunglasses;
of condemned men
that make me think
death comes in gusts—

their hats fly off as
the bullets floor them
with a final realization.
Stilled at last, they
seem completed.
It's the photo of a woman
that stops me.
She leans from the
cab of a train.
Her eyes are dark
as she hurtles through
the smoking, blasted
wreck of Mexico.
Her shawl cups the wind
as she stares through the room,
stares north while the waiters
hurry up with our food.

Men Waking

(the Ranchero Mobile Home Court in
Tatum, New Mexico)

Wind scars through the court.
Weed-trash hisses at elms
and the elms shush back as
these stalled trailers rock—
their curtains whipping metal.

Inside, the veneers
glass over and roll
with TV snow, with
a light that helps
wash down the years of
men whose elbows
scrawl divans,
whose soiled heads
bruise their pillows.

Where are the homecomings,
the wives and shared nights,
the sons they lifted
into daylight?

The sun shunts up the
riveted tin and
each trailer bumbles
with cold, sleep-heaving
brakemen, plumbers,
truckmen, riggers

getting ready
for daylight to harden
into what they will do.

FOUR

When You Took Your Luggage—

your long black hair and
the bus out of town
I clouded roads
with my Chevy's dust
and steered
both thumbs sticking up
cut by pop top cans of beer

The warm thick feel of
my blood on the wheel
I yelled the radio's Top Ten
and the moon
like the face of
a hit-and-run
rode my windshield
into town
into my eight by eleven room
into my sleep

Older

No long kissing anymore
No smoked roads through green nights
    I sang in
No dreams that chorused me awake
with whirrings of pages
with fast voice-overs
briefing me on all I would live through

Just the same slow wake
the coming-to in silence

Elegy for Paula

(1947-1979)

I say her name
to the still dark.
I say her name and
the four walls flicker
with my electric heater.
Like a medium
I hold hands with the dead,
beg the dead I have loved
to conspire, conspire,
and body her forth.
I hold hands with two
stillborn children,
a suicide,
a coronary.
Truman, William
and the unnamed—
they gather around me.
Eight lost hands stir
the air with my longing.

Late at night you may feel
a light bulb flicker
or a wall shudder.
Don't be afraid.
It's the dead's Morse code
tapping out messages
from one of the living
whose arms will never
reach through her silence.

Calming My Daughter

Rain breaks on the house
and you call me—
call through the dark
where I find you deep
in the well of the crib,
your fists wincing at
each shudder of thunder.

I rock you, mock your
frightened gibberish,
dangle words
above your eyes
until they ease.

Close, our faces
shine like signs while
the roots of night
downshift to nowhere.

* * *

A life from now
rock me, too.
Shake the bright,
helpless mobile
of our talk
when my eyes grow
too weak to reach.

Night-watching with My Daughter

You're up again and
pad to me while
I fidget and adjust
a telescope propped
in the cold backyard.
Caught for an instant,
a star strobes around
in the shaky lens,
holds briefly—
then my wrist aches
and the star fires off
like a lit match,
leaving framed blackness.
Red-ended, glowing,
you jostle between
me and the lens,
climb to my arms
and I haul us back
to our separate sleep.

Uirsche Endures a Weariness that Passes All Understanding

My sleep fills with thick tables of salt
popping miles down in the hot dark.
My dreams clot with fossils, oil,
twist like a grimace into the mornings.

Awake in the dark, I tell my lost daughter
how a fist of coal loved a diamond;
how the diamond loved a dying star;
how the star yearned back to the pinpoint
of absolute nothing.

"They died and, somehow, were happy forever."
The ceiling watches.
I exhale, perspire.
Ribcage and sinew rehearse their extinction.

The boxfan stirs my sister's letters.
The empty envelopes circle the room.
She writes that she weeps at a TV commercial
where a child steps off a set of scales
into the arms of its mother.

If I could groan past the crush of my life
to an easy moment, I would answer my sister:
*"I wish for a place to watch my child
until she steps off into the dark,
into my arms."*

FIVE
(Epilogue)

Uirsche on Circling

When the rest home voices
echo above me
I squint to those sharp
ceramic bells— then
collapse back to my
rapt ball of dream.
Again, my hands clinch
the wheel of my Ford
and I bear right on
this city loop
that is now my life.
I glance down to
the green ditch where
I played as a boy,
circle the lights of
this changeless, nearing
town of my joy:
the porch light of
my first apartment;
the streetlamp near
my childhood home;
the sun-banked windows
of East Ward High. When
I glance to the left
I see black nothing,
windless and starless.
The loop tightens.
My car veers through
the faces, moments:
my shirtless sister
squeals from the top
of her backyard swing;

Father—all dark
hands and anger—
shambles toward me;
Mother, her hair a
wispy corona 'round
the sun of her smile.
The highway sharpens
to a stop and I watch
as Shiela, me, and Larry
weave arm-in-arm through
the parking lot at
Nevelson's Deli.
I'm on the left.
As I turn to look back
my free hand lifts from
the cuff of my night-black
fireman's jacket.
I'm twenty-three,
giddy and clear on
sunlit January air,
and I wave as it
brightens brightens
and chars us to nothing.

Dreaming Back to the Barrio / 1954

Crossed popsickle sticks
fastened with string . . .
They jerk again in
the alley wind above
the brief graves of birds.

The years have taken me out how far?

I close my eyes and
the sticks jerk again,
in the hot weeds again,
behind the shame-faced shacks
blanking in the sun.

As I fall asleep
dark arms pass me down
to my better life.

Eight Hundred and Fifty copies printed
February 1988